Math = Fun!™

Shapes and Patterns

by Jerry Pallotta
Illustrated by Rob Bolster

SCHOLASTIC INC.

New York   Toronto   London   Auckland   Sydney
Mexico City   New Delhi   Hong Kong   Buenos Aires

Thank you to Andrea and Nichole Santoro.
—*Jerry Pallotta*

Dedicated to people who work hard.
—*Rob Bolster*

Text copyright © 2007 by Jerry Pallotta.
Illustrations copyright © 2007 by Rob Bolster.
All rights reserved. Published by Scholastic Inc.
SCHOLASTIC, Math = Fun!, and associated logos
are trademarks of Scholastic Inc.

ISBN-13: 978-0-545-00240-0
ISBN-10: 0-545-00240-0

12 11 10 9 8 7 6 5 4 3 2 1   7 8 9 10 11 12/0

Printed in the U.S.A.
This edition first printing, September 2007

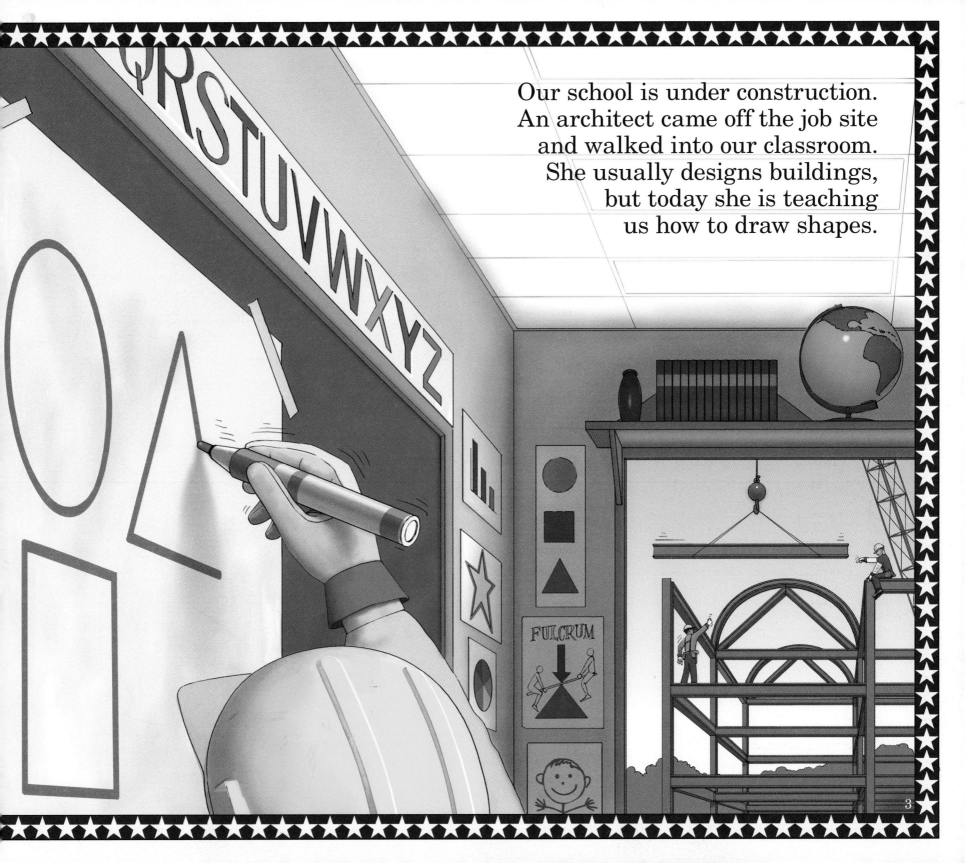

Our school is under construction.
An architect came off the job site
and walked into our classroom.
She usually designs buildings,
but today she is teaching
us how to draw shapes.

FULCRUM

3

point

line

The architect drew a dot and told us
it was a point in space.
We knew it was just a dot on the chalkboard.
Then she drew away from the dot to make a line.

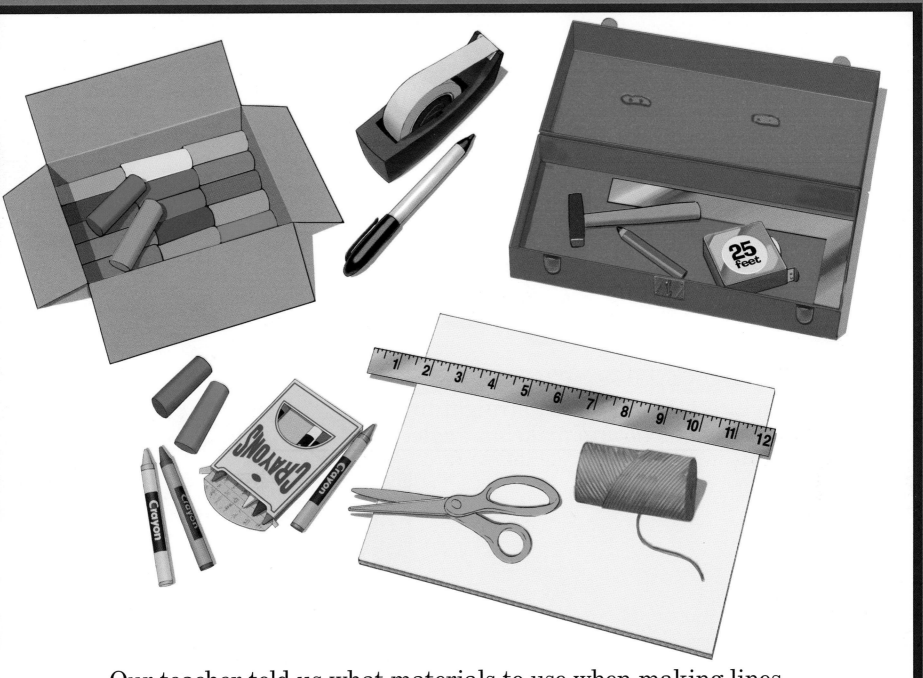

Our teacher told us what materials to use when making lines.
We can use pens, pencils, rulers, crayons, tape, paper, and scissors.
We can also use sidewalk chalk and string.

angle

The architect drew another straight line.
She showed us how to make an angle.

angle

wide angle

Then she drew more lines, and we learned about wide angles and skinny angles.

skinny angle

The first shape the architect showed us was a triangle.
It has three sides and three angles.
I made a triangle with crayons. It was really fun. I love to learn!

Outside at recess, we pretended we were architects
and construction workers. I remembered to wear my hard hat.
We colored on the playground with sidewalk chalk and drew triangles.

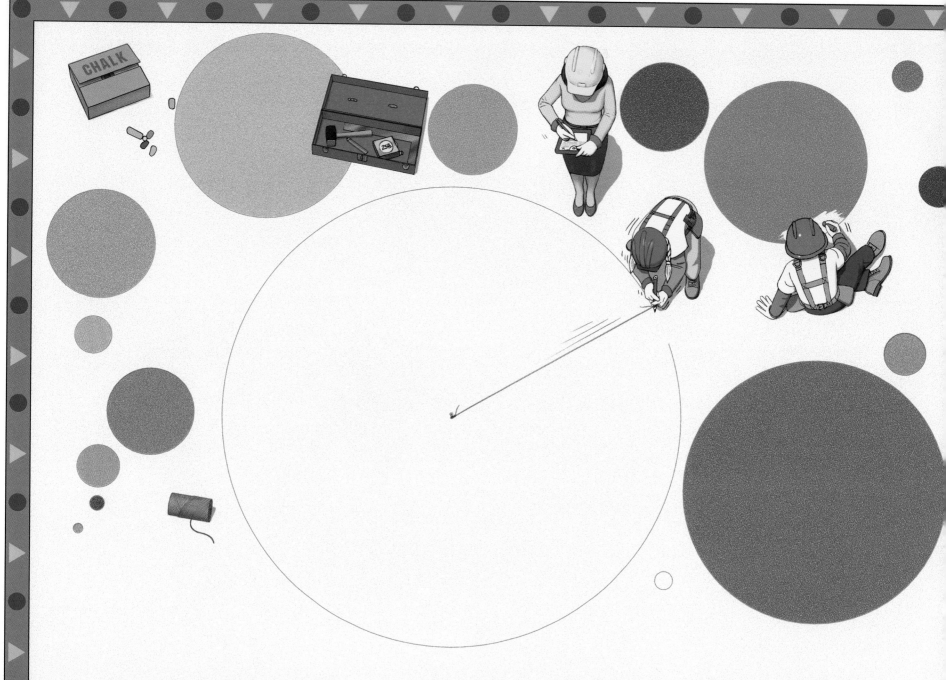

The next shape we learned about was a circle. The architect drew a dot. Then she helped us draw a curved line around it. The distance between the dot and the curve must be the same all the way around.

circle

My classmates and I made more circles. We colored some of them.

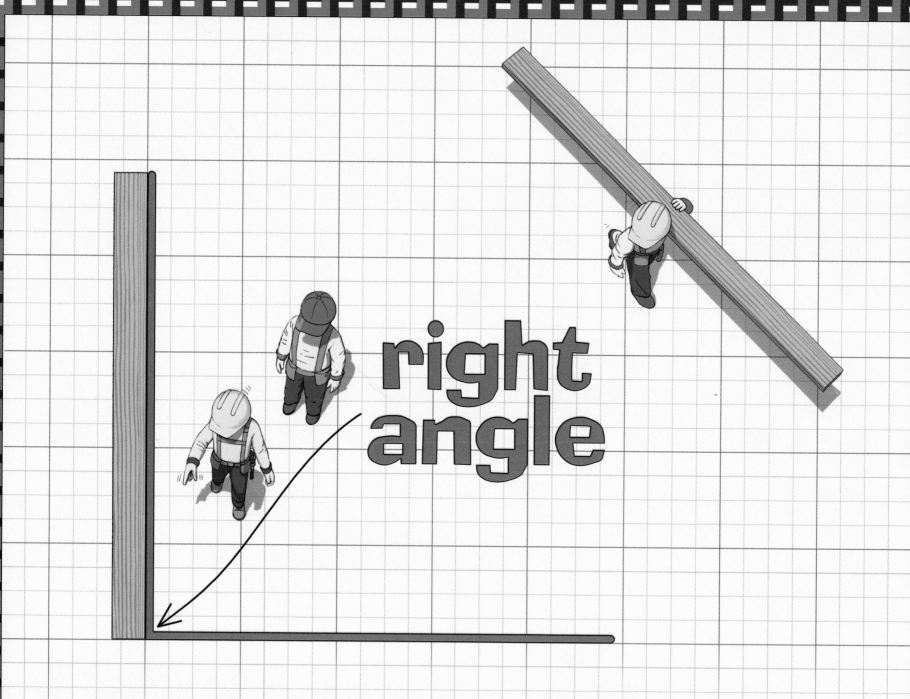

right angle

The architect took out some fancy graph paper to help us draw a right angle. The corner of this book is a right angle.

parallel lines

We learned about parallel lines.
Lines that are the same distance from each other
and do not touch are called parallel lines.

Learning about parallel lines and right angles is important!
Here is a square. A square is a four-sided shape with two pairs of parallel lines.
All four sides are the same length. All four angles are right angles.

Out on the playground, we tried to trick our teacher.
One of the shapes that we drew was not really a square.
Can you figure out which one is different?

This is not a circle. It is an oval. Ovals are egg-shaped.
You could say that an oval looks like a circle that has been stretched or squished.

Race cars drive on oval-shaped tracks.
The jogging tracks around football fields are oval-shaped.
Can you think of other ovals?

rectangle

Rectangles are everywhere. The architect told us to look at doors and windows. A rectangle has four straight lines and four right angles just like a square — but only the two sides opposite each other are the same length.

Think about this: A square is a rectangle,
but a rectangle is not always a square.
Our class could not decide which type is their favorite —
short, fat rectangles or really long, skinny rectangles.

pentagon

A shape with five sides is called a pentagon.
This pentagon has five equal sides and five equal angles.

Here is a diamond, a home plate, a kite, and an "I-don't-know-what-to-call-it!"
These are polygons. A shape with straight lines and more than
three sides is a polygon. The crescent moon and the heart are shapes, too.
But they are not polygons. They have curved lines.

Count the sides of this shape. One, two, three, four, five, six. Now count the angles. One, two, three, four, five, six. This polygon is called a hexagon.

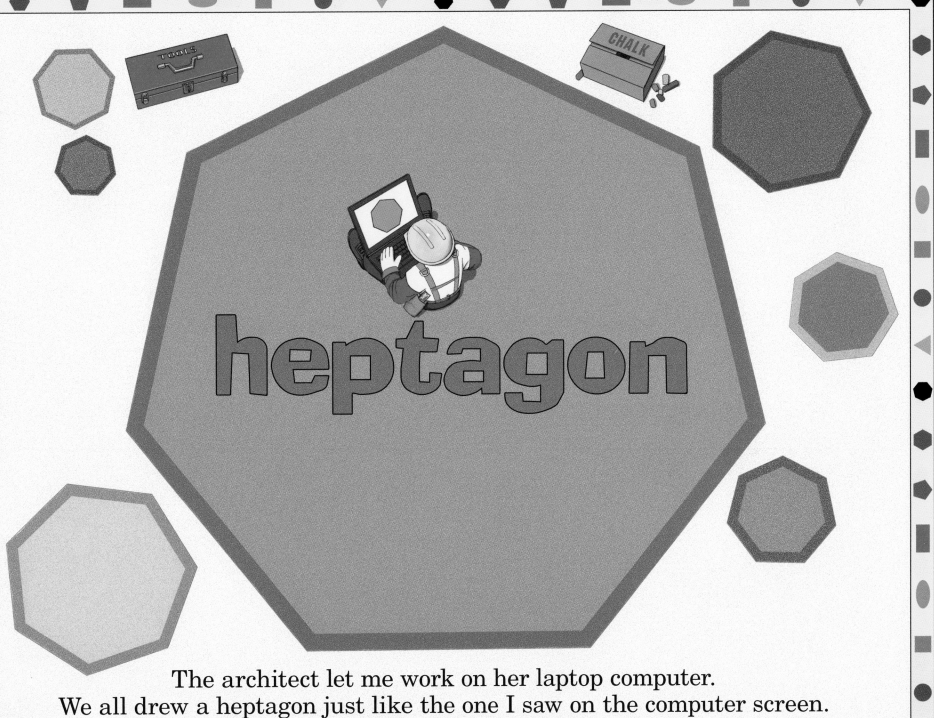

The architect let me work on her laptop computer.
We all drew a heptagon just like the one I saw on the computer screen.
A heptagon has seven sides.

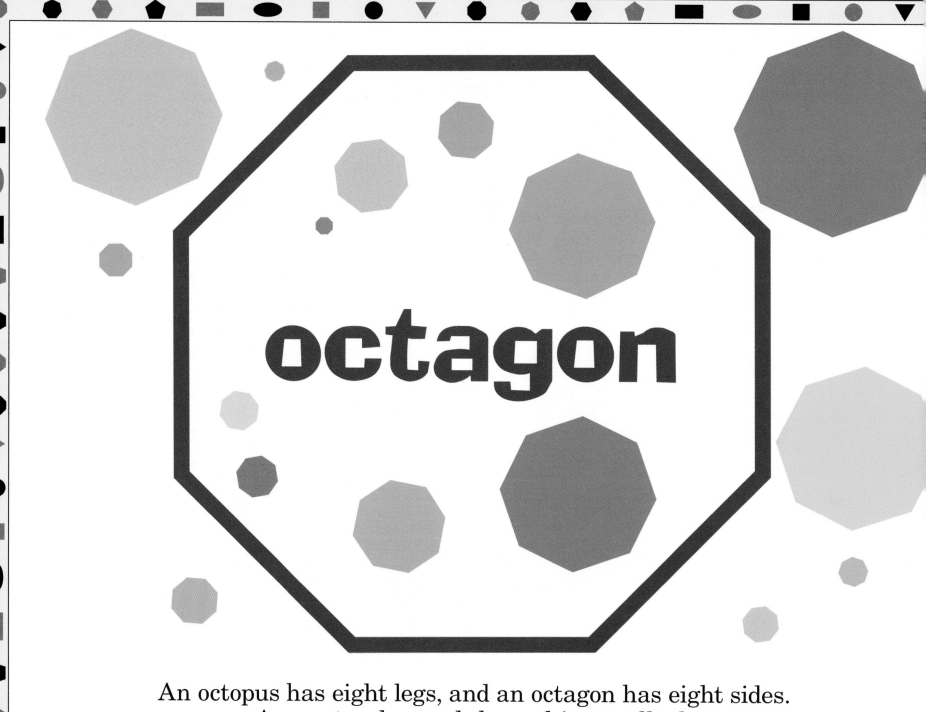

octagon

An octopus has eight legs, and an octagon has eight sides.
As our teacher and the architect talked,
I realized we could draw hundreds and hundreds of different shapes.

A nonagon has nine sides. Our whole class tried to think of a nonagon
in our town or near our school. We couldn't think of any.
Maybe for homework, our parents can help us find one.

decagon

A decade is ten years long. A decagon has ten sides.
We alternated the colors — red, blue, red, blue, red, blue, red, blue, red, blue —
to make this shape. Our teacher told us we were making a pattern.

Here is another pattern.
One blue dot, two green dots, one blue dot,
two green dots, one blue dot, two green dots.

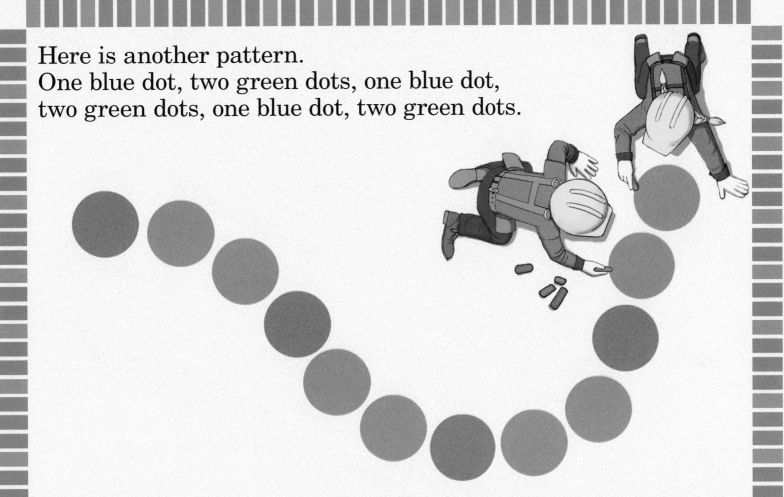

All but one of the patterns on this page go "one, two, one,
two, one, two." Can you find the different pattern on this page?

And how about this:
two boards, two steel beams, two boards, two steel beams.
I guess you could call this a "two-two" pattern.

I like this pattern the best: three red,
one blue, three red, one blue, three red.

Or you could say, three triangles, one oval,
three triangles, one oval, three triangles, one oval.
What would come next?
This is a "three-one" pattern.

Here is one more pattern: one board, green chalk, one steel beam,
space, one board, green chalk, one steel beam, space.
We made two shapes using this pattern.

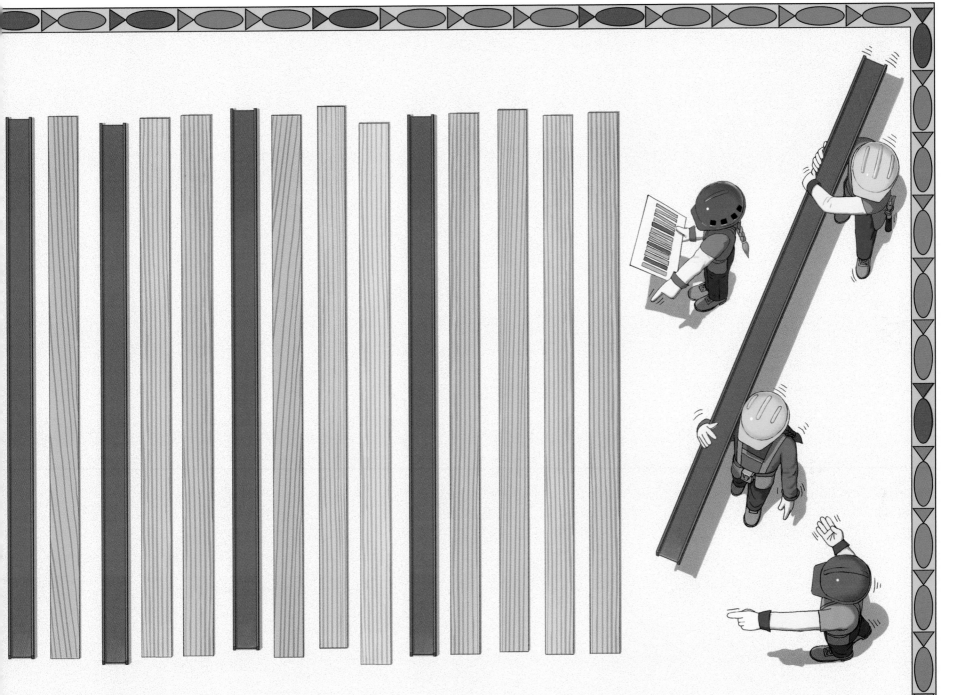

I have decided not to tell you any more. Figure this pattern out for yourself.
It is really cool. Go back and look at all the borders
in this book. There are patterns everywhere. Which page do you like the most?

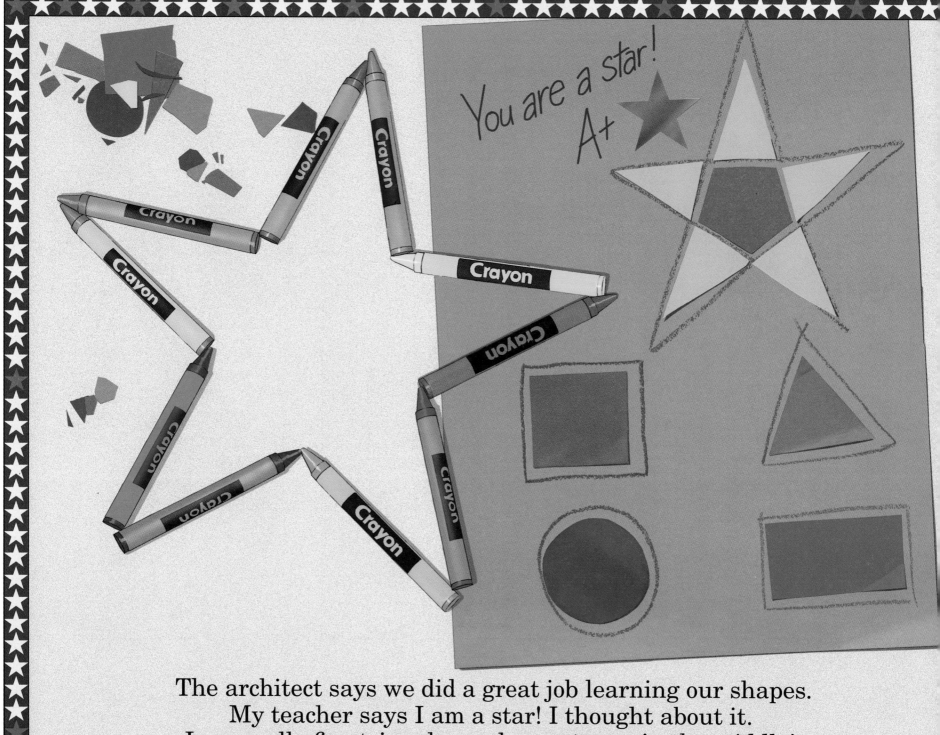

The architect says we did a great job learning our shapes.
My teacher says I am a star! I thought about it.
I am really five triangles and a pentagon in the middle!